An Engineer's Guide to MATLAB®